Clarity and Light

Clarity and Light

Meditations on Scripture

JESSE BAKER

RESOURCE *Publications* • Eugene, Oregon

CLARITY AND LIGHT
Meditations on Scripture

Copyright © 2025 Jesse Baker. All rights reserved. Except for brief quotations in critical publications or reviews, no part of this book may be reproduced in any manner without prior written permission from the publisher. Write: Permissions, Wipf and Stock Publishers, 199 W. 8th Ave., Suite 3, Eugene, OR 97401.

Resource Publications
An Imprint of Wipf and Stock Publishers
199 W. 8th Ave., Suite 3
Eugene, OR 97401

www.wipfandstock.com

PAPERBACK ISBN: 979-8-3852-4683-0
HARDCOVER ISBN: 979-8-3852-4684-7
EBOOK ISBN: 979-8-3852-4685-4
VERSION NUMBER 06/27/25

All Scripture quotations unless noted otherwise are taken from the New Revised Standard Version Bible, copyright 1989 by the Division of Christian Education of the National Council of Churches of Christ in the United States of America. Used by permission. All rights reserved.

Scripture quotations taken from The Holy Bible, New International Version, NIV. Copyright 1973, 1978, 1984, 2011 by Biblica, Inc. Used by permission. All rights reserved worldwide.

To Alison, Kellen, and Micah
My favorite future lovers of poetry

Then God said, "Let there be light"; and there was light. And God saw that the light was good; and God separated the light from the darkness. (Genesis 1:3-4)

They feast on the abundance of your house,
  and you give them drink from the river of your delights.
For with you is the fountain of life;
  in your light we see light. (Psalm 36:8-9)

Again Jesus spoke to them, saying, "I am the light of the world. Whoever follows me will never walk in darkness but will have the light of life." (John 8:12)

And the city has no need of sun or moon to shine on it, for the glory of God is its light, and its lamp is the Lamb. (Revelation 21:23)

Contents

Preface | xi

Acknowledgments | xiii

PROLEGOMENON
Clarity and Light | 3

THE OLD TESTAMENT
I. Torah

Good | 7

The Twirling Oak | 8

Hobbled | 9

Big Picture | 10

The God of Life | 11

Water Breaker | 12

Holy Ground | 13

Passover Promise | 14

Till Fear Is Gone | 15

A Full Cup | 16

Withholding | 17

Taste and See | 18

Moses' Spiritual Imagination | 19

II. The Writings and Wisdom

Blessed to Be a Blessing | 23

The Word Is My Shepherd | 24

A New Creation | 25

Sanctuary | 26

Heard and Seen | 27

Heaven Come Down | 28

Lamenting Leviathan | 29

A Night Not All Unwelcome | 30

Legacy | 31

Thoughts on Ecclesiastes | 32

When I Said "I Love You | 33

III. The Prophets

A House That Stands | 37

Decked and Adorned | 38

Looking in the Quiet | 39

Where Is the Lord? | 40

A New David | 41

A Song of Restoration | 42

A New Covenant | 43

Hope | 44

THE NEW TESTAMENT
I. The Gospel

Wonder | 47

Epiphany | 48

Fulfilled | 49

Beloved Son | 50

A Seventh Vessel | 51

The Call | 52

Empty Hands | 53

A New Teaching | 54

Salvation | 55

Blessed... How? | 56

Symbols | 57

The Great (Re)Commission | 58

The Sower | 59

Be Patient | 60

The Mustard Tree | 61

Unveiled | 62

As If | 63

The Choice | 64

The Good Editor | 65

Repentance | 66

A Son Among the Stars | 67

The Shepherd | 68

Do Not Be Terrified | 69

Being Ready | 70

Resembling the King | 71

The True Way into Life | 72

An Easter Lament | 73

A Friend Like Thomas | 74

Seeing Jesus | 75

Sitting | 76

II. Epistles

Half-life | 79

The Eighth Day | 80

Galatians | 81

Stilling the Storm | 82

III. Apocalypse

Reading Revelation | 85

On Words | 86

Heaven: Source and Center | 87

Preface

The poems in this collection were born out of pastoral need, both on an individual and communal level. As a pastor, several years ago I found myself in a sermonic writing rut of the worst kind. While I was never short on background information for a given text or help from commentaries, I had trouble finding a way to bring those ideas to life or make them meaningful for the church. Which brings me to the communal problem. I feared I wasn't giving my church members what they needed in our worship context. What I had was fact-heavy sermons with little to ignite the heart or inspire a spiritual imagination.

It was around this time that I rediscovered poetry. In the distant past I told myself I liked to write poetry, but after a bad poetry class in college (which I eventually dropped), I left all such notions behind. But after coming across poetry in a graduate class and finding the work of Malcolm Guite, ideas started firing. In fact, inspired by some of Guite's meditations on Scripture, I decided one week to write a poem as part of my sermon preparation process. I did, in fact, write a poem and, further, that poem helped me in writing that particular sermon. As it turns out, that initial poem was not all that great. I had no grasp of rhythm or meter, which is of course not helpful when trying to write metrical sonnets. (In other words, that poem is not in this collection.) But I started to wonder: what if I tried this process every week? So I gave it a shot. Now, and for the last several years, I have chosen a text, studied the text, written a poem based on that work, and lastly finished by writing a sermon based on that poetic reflection.

Preface

The majority of the poems in this collection were born out of that Scriptural meditation. As such, these poems are unapologetically devotional in nature. Not only has this process been helpful for me, but it has proven to be a helpful teaching tool in my church. To be sure, not everyone in my church is a lover of poetry. But since nearly one-third of the Bible is poetry (not to mention an even larger portion which, broadly speaking, uses poetic language), I am trying to give the average church member some window into the poetic mindset of many of the Biblical authors. And even though I build sermons from these poems, I also hope the poems themselves have an aura of a sermon; that they do what good sermons do and invite people to explore the Scriptures a little more deeply, that readers may encounter God as a result. Ultimately, I hope this process helps church members to live a little more wisely in the world, that the world in turn may encounter the goodness of God by the light of Jesus shining through his followers. Hence, I hope this book helps provide readers with both *clarity and light*.

I am indebted to many friends who helped bring this book to light (pun intended). Lee Kiblinger, Lee S. Kohman, Tyler Rogness, Joy E. S. Manning, and Becky Hunsberger each spent a few months combing through this collection, giving guidance on how to strengthen individual poems and helping me think about the shape of the collection. Heather Cadenhead also read an early draft and offered many good reflections on these poems. There many other poets and writers from The Habit, a community of writers led by Jonathan Rogers, who offered kind words and gave space for reading and critique. I consider this book a team victory, and I'm grateful for every bit of encouragement my friends have given along the way.

I am thankful to church members who have been kind and supportive of my writing efforts, even when they were the recipients of really bad poems.

Lastly, I am thankful for my wife Alison and my sons Kellen and Micah, who never minded too much when I spend a lot of time meditating by staring out of the window from my favorite chair or going for walks to think ideas through. Each of you is an inspiration.

Acknowledgments

On top of the people I mentioned in the Preface I am also grateful for the writing friends and journals who have previously published some of my work. They include:

"Good," first published in *Radix Magazine*. Vol. 43, No. 1.

"A Son Among the Stars," first published in *Habitations*, Volume 1

"Clarity and Light," "The Twirling Oak," and "Lamenting Leviathan," first published in *Habitations*, Volume 2

"The Mustard Tree" and "Stilling the Storm," first published in *Habitations*, Volume 3

"Hobbled," originally published in Issue #6: "Quiescence" by *The Clayjar Review*

"Legacy," "Where Is the Lord?," and "Symbols," first published in Issue #3: "A Great Light" by *The Clayjar Review*

"A Night Not All Unwelcome" was shared on the blog *Stories of Yearning* (in a series titled "Winter Eyrie") by Alicia Pollard

"Thoughts on Ecclesiastes," first shared by *The Rabbit Room Poetry* Substack.

The poems "A New Creation," "Moses' Spiritual Imagination," "The Good Editor," and "Being Ready" were included within the article "Poetic Pastoring: Using Poetry in Preaching" on *The Rabbit Room Poetry* Substack.

Prolegomenon

CLARITY AND LIGHT

...for darkness is as light to you. (Psalm 139:12)

When I sit down to write, I'm well aware
How little I can say I really know.
The page that stares at me insists the same:
It's bright, but blank. Light glimmers off the sheet
Reminding me there's work to do. To learn
What needs to be discerned will mean that white
Will need to be destroyed with darkness—strokes
Of ink penned in pursuit of deeper sight.
What I don't know, you know completely. I
Am asking you to take my hand and help
Me scribble truths within this opened book.
Since darkness is as day to you, I pray
The dark marks on these pages bring to me,
And all who read them, light and clarity.

The Old Testament
I. Torah

GOOD

... and indeed, it was very good. (Genesis 1:31)

Good, better, best: How we often suggest
What we have and what we finally long for.
We start with the tolerable, want more,
And in time reach our destination: best.
I wonder if a reevaluation
Is needed. Better and best are, at best,
Relational terms, and can start with "bad" just
As well as "good." Better's a promotion
From something worse; best is all we can do
In worst-case scenarios. We've turned
The world on its head and thereby churned
Up false expectations. Should we review
This dis-order, confess we've misunderstood?
Reset our aim where God began, with good?

THE TWIRLING OAK

Out of the ground the Lord *God made to grow every tree that is pleasant to the sight. (Genesis 2:9)*

I've slowed my pace or simply stopped and stared
countless times at the willow oak on Davis Street,
that, based on its twisted bark, burst from the ground
with a counterclockwise momentum.
Each time I pause to ponder this oddity
my mind moves waltz-like to the image of a dance,
where God takes the branchy hands of his
partner and twirls her round and round, full of grace.
It's my way of imagining that this tree is no accident
of soil or seed or springtime weather,
but one expression of how the joy of creation
is shared with the world. And who knows?
If a day really is like a thousand years to God,
perhaps this is one place where his timeless world
meets us in the here and now; the hundred-plus
years of growth is but a moment
currently unfolding to him. And that may be why
I stop on Davis Street so often.
I'm praying I might catch a glimpse
of that eternal world and this eternal dance,
hoping to hear God speak contentedly to his dance partner,
through roars of giddy laughter, *Oh, this is good.*

HOBBLED

Then the man said, "You shall no longer be called Jacob, but Israel, for you have striven with God and with humans, and have prevailed." (Genesis 32:28)

It reads as if the two came to a draw,
As neither walked away leaving his foe
Defeated in the dust. The stranger asked
The name of Jacob and, for once, he set
Aside deception, telling truthfully,
"My name's Deceiver; One Who's Crooked; Bent.
I've tripped the heels of all ahead of me,
Yet still have found myself possessing nothing."
To which his God responded, *Child, you'll learn
My blessing only comes upon the broken,
Upon the ones who've sought to bend my will
To theirs. They all leave marked, and sometimes bruised,
But always hobbling; so when they walk
With stuttered steps, they'll learn to lean on me.*

BIG PICTURE

But when his brothers saw that their father loved him more than all his brothers, they hated him, and could not speak peaceably to him. (Genesis 37:4)

The main character in the drama is Yahweh.
- WALTER BRUEGGEMANN

Keep on, dear reader. If you dropped in here
For just this story, you may think I'm absent,
Or standing off, aloof from all the action.
You might conclude, with just this tale, that I
Am punishing this once deceptive dad
With more deception, or I'm sending off
A bratty child that he might learn some manners.
But I assure you: none of these are true.
I wend within events in ways your eyes
Cannot now see. My sons are prone to stray;
But I have loving hands, and I can steer
Them gently where they need to go. I know
My children haven't acted as they should.
Read on. You'll see I'll turn it all for good.

THE GOD OF LIFE

"And now do not be distressed, or angry with yourselves, because you sold me here; for God sent me before you to preserve life."
(Genesis 45:5)

Is this not like our God? His ways are far
Above our own, his plans beyond what we
Conceive. Your hearts were set on harm.
You tossed Me in the pit to let the waves of death
Encompass me, and carry me away.
Yet God stepped in and calmed the swells. And while
Footprints were then unseen, now looking back
I see that only he could part those seas
To open up the way that led me here.
So do not be distressed. You buried me
To die, but God received me as a seed.
He gave it growth, and I've been lifted up
Not just for my own sake, but yours, and all
Who would come after, so that Abram's tree
Might grow and give the world its blessèd fruit.

WATER BREAKER

She named him Moses, "because," she said, "I drew him out of the water." (Exodus 2:10)

I see you, Daughter, and your desperate
Attempt to save your child. I know the words
Of Pharaoh shook you like a violent storm,
Like winds that whip the waves upon your shore.
I know it seems there may not be a choice
But to submit to death, to place your son
Within its hands and hope a miracle
Will draw him out from water's clammy grip.
Hush, do not fear. I will be with him as
He passes through the waters. I will lift
Him up to be a Water Breaker, just
The first of many sons who'll stand upon
The brink and call to me with their whole heart,
"Lord, let there be a way that leads to life."

HOLY GROUND

Then he said, "Come no closer! Remove the sandals from your feet, for the place on which you are standing is holy ground." (Exodus 3:5)

I'm asking you to look beyond this present
Moment, inviting you to reimagine
Your people's possibilities, and more,
My aim for all the earth. This bush is just
A taste of what I long to do; I want
My whole creation radiating with
My glory—every person, beast, and plant
Engulfed in my divine vitality.
So first, remove the sandals from your feet.
Take off those deadened skins and sink your toes
Deep in what once was arid dust but I've
Remade as garden soil. Soak in its life,
Imprint it everywhere you step so that
All other ground will dance with heaven's flame.

PASSOVER PROMISE

"And when your children ask you, 'What do you mean by this observance?' you shall say, 'It is the Passover sacrifice to the LORD.'" (Exodus 12:26-27)

Just as this night is shrouded thick in darkness,
So you are clothed with care. And soon you'll be
Enveloped in a tale that turns the tables
On this Egyptian tyrant who assumes
He owns the children I have called. So sit
On seats' sharp edge, and eat in haste. Recall
Your years of bitterness, but know: before
The dawn of day, you'll sing new songs of praise.

And when your children ask you, "Why this meal?"
Enfold them in this day; enrapture them
With songs of victory. And give them eyes
To see they've been en-storied with a God,
Whose loving hands will always gently guide
His children up to regions of delight.

TILL FEAR IS GONE

But Moses said to the people, "Do not be afraid, stand firm, and see the deliverance that the L<small>ORD</small> *will accomplish for you today; for the Egyptians whom you see today you shall never see again. The* L<small>ORD</small> *will fight for you, and you have only to keep still." (Exodus 14:13-14)*

Within a scene as grand as this, it's strange
The voices I relate to most are those that cry
In fear to Moses—those who doubt the change
Will do them good, and those who think they'll die
There in the wilderness. It's odd to say
There's comfort in the status quo when it
Can only lead to death. But death today
Makes "death delayed" seem like the better script.

I likewise fear and search for ways to hide
Myself, ignoring all your words, the signs
Revealing how you fight for me and guide
Me through the tides of time. Lord, redefine
My darkened heart and help my soul be stilled.
Till fear is gone and true faith is instilled.

A FULL CUP

"You are not to take up the name of YHWH for emptiness" (Exodus 20:7, translation from Everette Fox's The Five Books of Moses)

My children and my sacred treasure, take
My name upon you. Bear its weight, uphold
It like a vessel filled with wine that all
The nations taste the goodness of your God.
For you were once beleaguered souls, a cup
That Egypt emptied, drinking to the dregs.
But I have filled your glass again with wine
That quenches and assuages every thirst.
So share this chalice with the world. Do not
Withhold an ounce from anyone. And if
Its bowl is drained, return at once to me,
And I will fill it full. Don't offer out
An empty cup. Don't give to them the lie
The well from which you drink will ever dry.

WITHHOLDING

The L<small>ORD</small> said to Moses, "I have seen this people, how stiff-necked they are." (Exodus 32:9)

If this was just the first—or best, the last—
Offense, perhaps we all could laugh it off
And chalk it up to childish innocence
That passes just as fast as it began.
If only. We, however, know this is
Their default, not some hapless accident:
A choice, a classic case of failure, like
The time your mother's hand reached out for fruit.
Alas, their necks are hard like Pharaoh's heart
And, therefore, do not turn as easily
As I would wish. If they would look to me,
Imagine all the treasures I would give.
Have I, at any point, withheld from them?
Will they, at every turn, withhold from me?

TASTE AND SEE

And [YHWH] said, "I will make all my goodness pass before you." (Exodus 33:18)

You cannot handle now all that I am.
You would be stepping on the surface of
The sun, immersed in light that feels like weight,
As if Mount Horeb fell on top of you.
I'll give a glimpse, a gloried glimmer of
My goodness—just a flash of what you'd find
If I revealed my whole self unto you.
The taste will always leave you wanting more.
But still, the glare that glances off my back
Will leave its mark on you. A mark to show
These darkened souls—those who abandoned me—
No lifeless calf could once compare
With what I will provide for all who yearn
For me, and long to see my shining face.

MOSES' SPIRITUAL IMAGINATION

But Moses said to [Joshua], "Are you jealous for my sake? Would that all the Lord's *people were prophets, and that the* Lord *would put his spirit on them!" (Numbers 11:29)*

While I appreciate the sentiment,
There is no need for jealousy on my
Behalf. The spirit is a gift, which I
Do not, by right, possess. Recall: God breathed
In Adam's flesh the breath of life, and Eve,
Through him, received the same. Do you not think
Our Lord desires to give the same good gift
To all their sons and daughters after them?
I wouldn't be surprised if one day God
Unleashed his spirit on humanity—
His wind and fire breezing through the land,
Emblazing every heart that longs for him.
They'll be like tents in which our Lord will rest,
And through them will the world, again, be blessed.

II. The Writings and Wisdom

BLESSED TO BE A BLESSING

That person is like a tree planted
   by streams of water,
which yields its fruit in season. (Psalm 1:3, NIV)

Oh, reader, understand the choice this psalm
Presents. You're either tree or chaff: a plant
That flourishes, or else a lifeless husk
That weighs less than the air it glides upon.
The issue wholly rides on rootedness.
The righteous person reaches deep in Scripture's
Rich soil for God's own ever-flowing streams,
And stakes his life on every drink and draught.

And while its right to celebrate this tree—
Its rootedness turned into blessedness—
The flourishing is not an end itself.
The world was made to be a garden grove
With trees swelling with fruit that bears God's life.
Stretch out your limbs that all may take and eat.

THE WORD IS MY SHEPHERD

"Even though I walk through the darkest valley,
  I fear no evil." (Psalm 23:4)

I've walked through shadowed valleys where darkness
Dripped thick, and I could scarcely see the ground
Beneath my feet. But in the air, I heard
A voice—behind, before—which echoed off
The hills, insisting I continue on.
It was the voice who led his people through
The parted sea; the liquid voice who urged
Them through the dry and barren wilderness;
It was the voice who calls to us and says,
Take up your cross and follow me; the voice
Who bids us on our trek to sit at table
That we might be refreshed—*Come; take and eat.*
This gentle voice will lead us through the dark.
Keep speaking, Word, and guide me into light.

A NEW CREATION

Create in me a clean heart, O God,
 and put a new and right spirit within me....
Deliver me from bloodshed, O God,
 O God of my salvation,
 and my tongue will sing aloud of your deliverance. (Psalm 51:10, 14)

I am awash in sin and overwhelmed
By my iniquity. I am like those
In Noah's day—I'm only evil all
The time. It's almost like I've been this way
From birth, with my transgressions swelling up
Like tidal waves that beat against the shores
Of my already broken heart. Mercy,
My God. Be gracious to this troubled soul.
Don't take your spirit from me, Lord. Instead,
Just like when time began, come blow your breath
Upon these floods of guilt; and somehow use
These waters not for judgment, but to cleanse
My unclean heart and make me new, and I
Will ever sing of your deliverance.

SANCTUARY

But when I thought how to understand this,
  it seemed to me a wearisome task,
until I went into the sanctuary of God;
  then I perceived their end. (Psalm 73:16-17)

We're never told what happened
in the sanctuary—what he might have seen
or heard—only that he walked out different
than how he had arrived. If I could guess,
I'd bet he entered in that sacred space
and found a quiet corner in which to stand,
then spoke his mind—likely in third person
rantings—and, like Job, tried to put God
in his place. Perhaps he talked himself breathless,
and in exhaustion slid his back
slowly down the wall, shrinking
to a squat. From that low place, I wonder if
he looked up and caught a glimpse of God
sitting with him, nodding in tender sympathy,
saying—not in words, so much—*I'm here.*
We'll see this through together.
I can't be sure; but, I do know that silence sometimes
is the key that unlocks the way to understanding.

HEARD AND SEEN

Your way was through the sea,
  your path, through the mighty waters;
  yet your footprints were unseen. (Psalm 77:19)

Appreciation is an understatement;
I revel here in the relationship.
You take from one who's utterly dependent
His accusations, every gibe and quip,
With patience lead him to the moment where
He takes a breath that parts his troubled seas
To help him see that you are with him there,
Though in that space your steps are still unseen.

And that is gift enough, to know that we
Can share our griefs. But greater grace is given
In Christ whose steps are seen; that we could see
Him come, as the embodiment of heaven,
And step into the storms where we have trod
And speak, "Be still, and know that I am God."

HEAVEN COME DOWN

I say, "You are gods,
  children of the Most High, all of you;
nevertheless, you shall die like mortals,
  and fall like any prince." (Psalm 82:6-7)

Within the Scriptures there are two ways heaven
Descends to earth. There is the psalm where gods
Are judged, humiliated for rejecting
Creation's fundamental goodness, choosing
Instead a world ruled by their own desires:
A world that cannot work and will not last,
As God is said to take his stand, revoke
Their life, that they may taste mortality.

And then there's Christ, who takes on human form.
Who, by his word and healing touch, freely
Shares everything he has, infusing all
Creation with the goodness that it lost,
That we who've only known a sinful stature
May now partake of his divine nature.

LAMENTING LEVIATHAN

... and Leviathan that you formed to sport in [the sea]. (Psalm 104:26)

There are several texts where you suggest
    that you delight to see the dragon frolicking about.
    You have that right, and I agree in the abstract.
However, I'm less inclined to join
    in your rejoicing while I'm floating on
        this lifeless boat, its wind-dead sails hanging limp.
I'm only moved—with dread—
    when waters ripple from the monster's slither, jostling
        my tiny boat, unsettling my seasick soul.
If it's all the same, I wish you'd tell this beast I'd rather be left alone.

A NIGHT NOT ALL UNWELCOME

Last night, amid the darkness,
I briefly stepped outside
To undo something forgotten;
And the full February moon,
Standing alone in the pitched sky,
Begged for my attention.
She reminded me of childhood
Nights, and how I would borrow
Her light as I walked to our
Chicken house, nestled in the trees
Down a darkened and wooded road,
To gather hen eggs.
She also brought to mind the
Wonder of those nights when
Her full light glimmered
Off the earth's snowy blanket,
Gently placed over previous days,
Giving me both a brighter path to tread and
Some glimpse of what the psalmist
Might have meant when he said, "The night is as
Bright as the day," to you.

LEGACY

"If your ambition is to leave a legacy, what you'll leave is a legacy of ambition." - RICH MULLINS

I've walked on sidewalks where people
have taken advantage of wet concrete
to imprint their presence and prowess
for all future pedestrians to see.
I've never had the opportunity
to leave such a mark, but
I'm also not sure I ever would.
I don't think well on my feet, and so
would have nothing in the moment
to write worth preserving. Even if I did,
my hyperconscious self would fear how others
might regard such an unknown artist.
The responsible thing to do, I would say,
would be to walk the long way around
and get on with the rest of the day.

I was stopped in my tracks the other day
while on my favorite park trail—
not too far from a bench given
in memory of someone's beloved Mary Young—
when I noticed footprints of a bird running
perpendicular to the path, fossilized
in the dry concrete. I found it hard to imagine
a bird looking over its left wing and facetiously
telling his friends this was his chance to
to cement his legacy for all time. I pictured
instead a bird concerned with food or nest building,
going about his mundane, daily tasks
and unknowingly leaving a lasting mark.

THOUGHTS ON ECCLESIASTES
(or, For the Love of Pipe Smoking)

The Teacher says all life is a vapor,
As if it has a scent like cigarette.
That life is like we're all walking through awned doorways
Crowded with smokers on a rainy day
Getting their quick nicotine fix,
While we, against our wills, are unmistakably marked
With their peculiar perfume.

I wonder what it would have been like
Had the Teacher been around pipe smokers,
Catching their aromatic sweetness—
A vapor not standing as a barrier
To Joy, but as a warm and welcome embrace
Into an experience of goodness.
Their smoke wafts and billows in the air,
like arms waving us to come close.
Almost as if to say,
Come, friend. Taste and see.

WHEN I SAID "I LOVE YOU

You have ravished my heart... (Song of Solomon 4:9)

On your couch, we sat close.
I don't recall the exact date,
but I know it was just a month or so
after we said we liked each other. I remember
I was sitting and you were lying down,
leaning in on me, with your head just below mine
which allowed me to rest my head on yours.
Again, it had only been a month or so, but
probably half that time I wondered if I should tell you.
I had no doubt, but wasn't sure if you would say it in return.
For me, speaking these three words into the air paved
the road ahead, and, I hoped, would bind our futures together.
So while I don't recall the exact date, what I know for sure
is when I said "I love you" twenty-one years ago
it meant that when we reached a day like today
I would love you still.

III. The Prophets

A HOUSE THAT STANDS

Your house and your kingdom shall be made sure forever before me; your throne shall be established forever. (2 Samuel 7:16)

Not now, my son. A house is not what I
Require. It may be you've become confused,
Assuming you must do for me as I
Have done for you. My child, I raised you from
The fields, and I subdued your enemies
On every side. I do not need your bricks;
I need a people who will trust that what
I did for you, I'll do for every age.

In days to come, it will appear that all
Is lost, as if the garden planted by
My hands is trampled with no sign that fruit
Will grow again. But those with ears to hear
Will know this promise holds, that even from
A stump, a tree that bears your name will come.

DECKED AND ADORNED

I will greatly rejoice in the Lord;
    my whole being shall exult in my God;
for he has clothed me with the garments of salvation;
    he has covered me with the robe of righteousness,
as a bridegroom decks himself with a garland
    and as a bride adorns herself with her jewels. (Isaiah 61:10)

Yes, all the world beheld your brokenness.
They saw your city crumbled, lying in
The dust. They've seen you decked in mourning garb,
Covered in ash, and visibly despondent.
They heard despairing cries and mocked as you
Cried out, "O Lord, how long?" And they sat back
In ease as you bewailed injustice done
While covenantal threads hung, dangling loose.

And so God's Spirit bids me stand and speak
Good news: Captivity is at its end;
A jubilee like none you've ever known
Is soon to come. And I will bring with me
God's robes of righteous white adorning you
With vestments marking his new victory.

A HOUSE THAT STANDS

Your house and your kingdom shall be made sure forever before me; your throne shall be established forever. (2 Samuel 7:16)

Not now, my son. A house is not what I
Require. It may be you've become confused,
Assuming you must do for me as I
Have done for you. My child, I raised you from
The fields, and I subdued your enemies
On every side. I do not need your bricks;
I need a people who will trust that what
I did for you, I'll do for every age.

In days to come, it will appear that all
Is lost, as if the garden planted by
My hands is trampled with no sign that fruit
Will grow again. But those with ears to hear
Will know this promise holds, that even from
A stump, a tree that bears your name will come.

DECKED AND ADORNED

*I will greatly rejoice in the L*ORD*;*
 my whole being shall exult in my God;
for he has clothed me with the garments of salvation;
 he has covered me with the robe of righteousness,
as a bridegroom decks himself with a garland
 and as a bride adorns herself with her jewels. (Isaiah 61:10)

Yes, all the world beheld your brokenness.
They saw your city crumbled, lying in
The dust. They've seen you decked in mourning garb,
Covered in ash, and visibly despondent.
They heard despairing cries and mocked as you
Cried out, "O Lord, how long?" And they sat back
In ease as you bewailed injustice done
While covenantal threads hung, dangling loose.

And so God's Spirit bids me stand and speak
Good news: Captivity is at its end;
A jubilee like none you've ever known
Is soon to come. And I will bring with me
God's robes of righteous white adorning you
With vestments marking his new victory.

LOOKING IN THE QUIET

O that you would tear open the heavens and come down,
  so that the mountains would quake at your presence. (Isaiah 64:1)

I know I've called you down. I've asked you, "Come
And intervene!" in troubling times. And like
The prophet what I really wanted then
Was something visible. Perhaps not heaven
Ripped open, but at least some sign that you
Were here. But never once have walls within
My house begun to shake, or light burst in
With force that pushed me crumbling to the ground.

But, then, I think that even in the Scriptures
It wasn't always so. Like when your Son,
Soon after seeing heaven rent, traveled
Judea's quiet corners, binding up
The broken one by one, and whispering
Into their ears, *The kingdom has arrived.*

WHERE IS THE LORD?

Be appalled, O heavens, at this,
  be shocked, be utterly desolate,
                              says the L<small>ORD</small>,
for my people have committed two evils:
  they have forsaken me,
the fountain of living water,
  and dug out cisterns for themselves,
cracked cisterns
  that can hold no water. (Jeremiah 2:12-13)

The prophet Jeremiah questioned why
His people had neglected asking, "Where,
Where is the Lord?", and thinking God was pleased
To dwell unbothered in his holy tent.
Instead, God longed to lead them from their deserts
For more Edenic springs on mountain tops,
And feed them with the fruit that grows unending
On trees which sprout by streams of living waters.
But as it was, they wanted none of these:
Content to live by work their own hands wrought,
Like broken cisterns leaking all their water,
Or lifeless shapes they call their deities.
The prophet uses words like wood or kindling
To reignite their hearts for God again.

A NEW DAVID

The days are surely coming, says the LORD, when I will raise up for David a righteous Branch, and he shall reign as king and deal wisely, and shall execute justice and righteousness in the land. In his days Judah will be saved and Israel will live in safety. And this is the name by which he shall be called: "The LORD is our righteousness."
(Jeremiah 23:5-6)

Did you forget about my servant David,
Called out from fields while tending sheep to be
Anointed shepherd of my people?
Did you forget to lead them to the feast
Prepared by my own hands—the land a table
Filled full with milk and honey, bread and wine?
Did you forget his broken, humble heart,
His life of prayer which sought my love and mercy?
Well, I have not forgotten these, and I'll
Replace you all with one who'll set things right.
This David will become the gateway back
To pleasant lands. He'll sing in soothing tones
To woo the scattered sheep to me, that all
May taste and see the goodness of their King.

A SONG OF RESTORATION

For thus says the Lord of hosts, the God of Israel: Do not let the prophets and the diviners who are among you deceive you, and do not listen to your dreams that they dream, for it is a lie that they are prophesying to you in my name; I did not send them, says the Lord. (Jeremiah 29:8-9)

I cannot fault the exiled Israelites
For latching on to prophecies that speak
Of less pain, fewer years in Babylon
(Even though none of this had God's approval).
It was a simple melody. One quick
To learn and easy on their eager ears.
It was the type of song they longed to hear
With major keys and no polyphony.

But Jeremiah sang a different tune,
One layered with complexity, but sung
In harmony with God who sang all things
To life. The prophet urged his kin
To join in singing songs of new creation
In Babylon, till time of restoration.

A NEW COVENANT

But this is the covenant that I will make with the house of Israel after those days, says the LORD: *I will put my law within them, and I will write it on their hearts; and I will be their God, and they shall be my people. (Jeremiah 31:33)*

It wasn't that the words themselves were wrong
And gave false guidance leading folks astray;
Or the amount of laws was insufficient,
Or failed to touch some part of daily life.
And no one claimed that God did not make clear
What he expected of his chosen bride.
It simply was they weren't obedient,
But shirked all God's demands for holiness.

The days that Jeremiah said were coming
Would fix the wrong within the broken system—
When God would enter into people's hearts
And with his finger write on fleshly tablets
The words of hope which speak of his forgiving,
And words of love that bring both life and blessing.

HOPE

In their presence I charged Baruch, saying, Thus says the L<small>ORD</small> of hosts, the God of Israel: Take these deeds, both this sealed deed of purchase and this open deed, and put them in an earthenware jar, in order that they may last for a long time. For thus says the L<small>ORD</small> of hosts, the God of Israel: Houses and fields and vineyards shall again be bought in this land. (Jeremiah 32:13-15)

It's hard to find this scene as anything
But strange. That while the armies of the north
Surround the city's edge and Jeremiah's
Confined for speaking God's confounding truths,
A word that bordered on absurd was told:
Go buy a plot of land. The deed, seed-like,
Was buried deep inside an earthen jar
To rest in time's both slow and steady hand.
But God then spoke again. *I give this sign*
As hope to bridge the gap between your loss
And your return to hearth and home. Though it
May seem eternity, you shall both buy
And sell once more within this land: A seed
I promise to nurture with my own hands.

The New Testament
I. The Gospel

WONDER

And she gave birth to her firstborn son and wrapped him in bands of cloth, and laid him in a manger, because there was no place for them in the inn. (Luke 2:7)

Did Mary feel frustration when she learned
She had to travel? Or, perhaps a sense
Of sadness that the simple acts of nesting
Were made impossible since she, herself,
Had been un-nested? Did she whisper prayers
In rhythm with their steady pace, begging
Birth pangs delay until arriving at
More pleasant dwellings? Did her heart sink down
When hearing she would have to sleep low in
The cellar stable? Did her fear spiral
With animals bleating, braying to match
Her birthing screams? And as the child was laid
Upon her chest, was all that came before
Forgotten when she held—beheld—new life?

EPIPHANY

In the time of King Herod, after Jesus was born in Bethlehem of Judea, wise men from the East came to Jerusalem, asking, "Where is the child who has been born king of the Jews? For we observed his star at its rising and have come to pay him homage." (Matthew 2:1-2)

The heavens, singing back to God
who sang them into being,
understandably changed their tune
to welcome a King's arrival
in an otherwise silent, small town.
Far offstage, men listened attentively,
hearing and heeding a call to join the exaltation.

Startled to find such well-traveled strangers
in their midst searching for a king,
scholars recalled this son of David
was known by a minor prophet
who broke from his minor key
to announce that God would one day restart
his joyful opus in a familiar place.

The strangers followed the song to its source,
fusing their own voices with the heavenly chorus,
to laud an (as-yet) unknown King.

FULFILLED

... what had been spoken ... (Matthew 2:15, 17, 23)

"Fulfill" is Matthew's favored term describing
Both how and why these wild and harried scenes
Unfold. Just like before, salvation comes
From Egypt, only now this One will lead
A greater exodus. No deeper wounds
Are known than when their so-called king takes on
The role of pharaoh, killing Rachel's children,
That he might keep his throne a little longer.
And in the no-name town of Nazareth
A seed begins to blossom; fruitfulness—
Unknown since David's day—will soon return.
The *nezer*—Branch—is growing from the stump
Where healing leaves begin to bud, a sign
That Eden's tree will bloom again in full.

BELOVED SON

And a voice came from heaven, "You are my Son, the Beloved; with you I am well pleased." (Luke 3:22)

Soon after God
announces Jesus as his Son—
both chosen and beloved—
Luke paints the family tree,
giving all with eyes to see
space to recall collective moments of success
and failure, of promise
and hard-won hope,
and maybe even inspire
a renewed desire
for a storied resolution.

Jesus—beloved and pleasure-giving—
prayed, set-apart, where God made clear
that he was chosen to entangle and entwine
his ram-like horns among those family branches
to rustle up their wind-dead leaves;
not so much to get away
from any future harm, but precisely so
the knife's edge might turn toward him—
that on that day, all may look to him and see
why it is that people will never cease to say,
"Upon the mount, the Lord has provided."

A SEVENTH VESSEL

Now standing there were six stone water jars for the Jewish rites of purification, each holding twenty or thirty gallons. Jesus said to them, "Fill the jars with water." And they filled them up to the brim.
(John 2:7-8)

He stood there still as stone,
while servants and disciples either leapt
for joy or looked around with hands on heads
and mouths agape. They all witnessed the six jars
filled, to the point where water hovered
slightly above the brims. And somehow, when
the dipper was inserted, a crimson liquid streaked
the side of the dusty vessel
and pooled a deep red on the ground
before it seeped its way into the earthen floor.
The wondrous bounty carried the servants away,
caught up in the moment, eager to share
this best-of-wines with every wedding guest.
But Jesus remained there in that quiet room—
motionless, like one of the jars—
with eyes and mind fixed farther down the road.
He stood there still as stone,
in a more somber state of joy,
seeing himself the seventh vessel,
waiting to overflow.

THE CALL

And he said to them, "Follow me, and I will make you fishers of people."
(Matthew 4:19)

And what is your response? He waits to hear.
The call was never meant to hang back there
In Galilee, but to resound across
The ages, reaching every heart and ear.
So what is your response? He bids you come
And join him on the road that runs from home,
From what's familiar to what's still unknown,
To lead you to the entrance of his kingdom.
And what if you refuse? You'll miss the Light.
The source who once divided day and night,
Who spoke and blessed the world with all its life,
Who says he'll heal the blind and give them sight.
He's come to bring the promised renaissance.
He's here and waiting. What is your response?

EMPTY HANDS

Immediately [Jesus] called them; and they left their father Zebedee in the boat with the hired men, and followed him. (Mark 1:20)

When these two later asked
to sit upon his right and left,
I wonder if (in private) Jesus
reminded them of this first meeting
and gently guided them to an understanding
that their request was yet another net
they needed to leave behind—
that there was still much good
our Lord desired to give them; but,
the only way they could receive it all
was reaching out with empty hands.

A NEW TEACHING

They were all amazed, and they kept on asking one another, "What is this? A new teaching—with authority! He commands even the unclean spirits, and they obey him." (Mark 1:27)

A classic case of *show, don't tell*. I'd guess
His new disciples weren't clued in on lesson
Plans, but were learning right along with all
The other pupils. Now, they may have known
His teaching was connected with "the kingdom"
He previously preached, but I assume
They were not very far in understanding what
That meant; so with the rest they watched and learned.
And what were the results? They saw a king
Coming to conquer Canaan yet again,
Coming to cleanse the world of wickedness,
Revealing heaven present in their midst,
In hope that all may here begin to see
The certain goodness God has come to bring.

SALVATION

As soon as they left the synagogue, they entered the house of Simon and Andrew, with James and John. Now Simon's mother-in-law was in bed with a fever, and they told [Jesus] about her at once. He came and took her by the hand and lifted her up. Then the fever left her, and she began to serve them. (Mark 1:29-31)

Salvation, yes,
but not some kind abstracted
from recipient or source, and not the kind
that could be anywhere or one day
will be everywhere.
No; salvation—here:
in a small room in an already
small house; and for a woman—
unnamed, but no less changed—
risen from the covers
that once held her captive,
and now bustling around her house
serving cupfuls of abundant life.

BLESSED... HOW?

"Blessed... for theirs is the kingdom." (Matthew 5:3)

I find that my initial hopes of being
Included in the category "blessed"
Are not as strong—are not as once appealing—
Discovering these "happy" are oppressed,
And mourning, thirsty, hungry, and reviled.
They're those who have been wronged, but chosen mercy,
Whose fiery trials have left them purified,
Who, when trampled, have learned humility.

I know this list is not, at first, inviting;
But sit with these strange words that I have spoken.
I give them to a world in need of healing,
To those who know its systems are all broken.
These words are seeds of hope that I am planting,
To later flourish in the world I'm bringing.

SYMBOLS

I wrote the letter "T" on the page and wondered
If I asked him what sound he made,
Would he respond,
"Oh, I make no sound, friend.
I was asked to stand here proudly,
Hat on my head, to simply remind you
Of the sound that is to be made"?

I told my wife I loved her
And caressed her head as I leaned
To give her a kiss. The quiet smack lingered
In the air, as if to say, "Ah, here is love.
Love that is often kept silent,
But was just expressed, the unseen and unheard
Overflowing into a world of sight and sound."

Early Sunday morning, bread and wine
Were placed on a table, and in due time
Lifted before the body while proclaiming "This is…"
I wondered: Was "This is" a pointer like the
Letter, or an expression like the kiss?
Having no time then to think it through,
I contented myself to break the bread and
Spoke to the people the words of our Lord,
"Blessed are those who hunger and thirst…
For they shall be filled."

THE GREAT (RE)COMMISSION

"You are the salt of the earth; but if salt has lost its taste, how can its saltiness be restored? It is no longer good for anything, but is thrown out and trampled under foot.
    "You are the light of the world. A city built on a hill cannot be hid. No one after lighting a lamp puts it under the bushel basket, but on a lampstand, and it gives light to all in the house. In the same way, let your light shine before others, so that they may see your good works and give glory to your Father in heaven." (Matthew 5:13-16)

When light first broke into the darkness, God
Laid out how every night would end, how all
The evils of this world would be exposed,
How Israel should understand their call.

When salt was sprinkled on their offering
They learned through this preservative that they
Had entered in a covenant, agreeing
Their bond would last for all eternity.

So on a mountain Jesus could proclaim
That all the crowd who stood there listening
Could, at that moment, hear and then reclaim—
To recommit to their commissioning,
To be, through Christ, a sign that night was ending,
To be the heralds of the kingdom's coming.

THE SOWER

And he told them many things in parables, saying: "Listen! A sower went out to sow..." (Matthew 13:3)

The sower casts his seed in sections where
No other sower would. It is endearing
To think a farmer had such high hopes he
Could turn his whole landscape into a garden,
Delighting all who might pass by. And I
Could see this farmer standing near his fields
Inviting all, with joy, to come partake
Of his abundant fruitfulness. But how
Precisely will he break the hardened ground?
He'll bend down on his hands and knees, and bring
His face close to the soil, so near that grains
Of dust blow up and cling onto his lips
As he breathes out and whispers winsome words,
Open to me and I will give you life.

BE PATIENT

"Let both of them grow together until the harvest; and at harvest time I will tell the reapers, Collect the weeds first and bind them in bundles to be burned, but gather the wheat into my barn." (Matthew 13:30)

This scene assumes some folks suggest the seeds
That Jesus says he's planting cannot be
Connected to God's kingdom, since there'd need
To be a judgment setting people free
From all oppressors, only leaving God's
Divine community. But here, the weeds
Remain among the wheat, and iron rods
Endure in tyrants' hands who won't concede.
So Jesus seeks to calm their anxious minds
With this small parable, explaining how
While farmers wait long months before they find
Ripe wheat, they trust the growth is happening now:
With every word, my kingdom's taking root,
And in due time, I'll gather all my fruit.

THE MUSTARD TREE

He put before them another parable: "The kingdom of heaven is like a mustard seed that someone took and sowed in his field; it is the smallest of all the seeds, but when it has grown it is the greatest of shrubs and becomes a tree, so that the birds of the air come and make nests in its branches." (Matthew 13:31-32)

It's said, "Christ plays in ten thousand places,"
And where he is, his kingdom's also there,
Beginning as a seed—one small enough
That if it fell upon the ground you'd have
To crawl down on your knees to find it; but,
If planted, nurtured, rooted deep within
The soil, becomes a tree which birds—like jays,
Kingfishers, gulls, and sparrows—make their home.
The songs they sing will ring like Sunday's bells,
Broadcasting joyfully in each of those
Ten thousand places, *Christ our Lord is here!*
Their sound resounds, alighting on the ears
An invitation: *Come, and rest. Come nest
Yourself within this tree's gentle embrace.*

UNVEILED

As they were coming down the mountain, Jesus ordered them, "Tell no one about the vision until after the Son of Man has been raised from the dead." (Matthew 17:9)

I've often thought that Jesus coming down
The mount, no longer luminescent, was
In some way like the scene at Sinai, where
We read that Moses hid his shining face
Since others found it hard to look at him.
And Jesus, full of grace, would know if Moses
Could not reveal a slanted glimpse of glory,
Then all the more his fullness must be veiled.

But knowing now the road that brought him down
The hill had signs all pointing to the cross,
Then each beleaguered step that Jesus took
Was not some strained attempt to shroud or hide,
But was his chosen means of revelation;
That in his death, his glory was unveiled.

AS IF

Then Peter said to Jesus, "Rabbi, it is good for us to be here; let us make three dwellings, one for you, one for Moses, and one for Elijah." He did not know what to say, for they were terrified. (Mark 9:5-6)

As if anything needed said. As if
The Father sat with bated breath waiting
For Peter's words to fill a void God's glory
Was ill-prepared to fit. As if our Lord
Required shrines to mark the time and place,
Perhaps setting the stage for later tours—
"You should have been there!" guides might say—as if
This sight itself was all that really mattered.

Listen to him was said to wake them from
Their fear-filled stupor, and to let them know
They had no way of understanding then
What happened there, and wouldn't till the day
That death's undone and all becomes more clear,
Re-visioned through the resurrection's light.

THE CHOICE

The crowds that went ahead of him and that followed were shouting,
  "Hosanna to the Son of David!
    Blessed is the one who comes in the name of the Lord!
   Hosanna in the highest heaven!"
When he entered Jerusalem, the whole city was in turmoil, asking,
"Who is this?" (Matthew 21:9-10)

Our story hinges on this crucial choice:
Either we stand within the walls and question
Who Jesus thinks he is, or we rejoice.
We either bristle at the crowd's expression,
Or we take up the song and sing his praise,
Proclaiming him as king for all our days.

O may I sing, on this and every day,
Hosanna!, sing with fullness of my being
This song of welcome. And may I then lay
My everything upon the ground, freeing
Myself from all that might prevent me
From offering my whole self unto you.
Please come, my gentle King, my Lord of mercy,
Come dwell in me and ever make me new.

THE GOOD EDITOR

"For which of you, intending to build... does not first sit down and estimate the cost?" (Luke 14:28)

The writer finds from time to time beloved
Ideas, phrases, words that stifle lively
Storytelling and have to be removed.
(Sometimes, we say, "our darlings have to die.")
I've never thought the process easy, but
I've seen the letting go lead to real growth,
As if aerating the creative soil
Allows a fresh wind to breathe in new life.

I wonder if our Lord here plays the role
Of editor by asking his disciples
To trust that he can show them how to tell
A better story. He suggests that they
Part ways with images they once held precious
To find what makes their story truly priceless.

REPENTANCE

"So he set off and went to his father. But while he was still far off, his father saw him and was filled with compassion; he ran and put his arms around him and kissed him." (Luke 15:20)

I know that Chesterton once wrote that you,
O God, have an eternal appetite
Of infancy, that each daisy and every
Sunrise offer unique beauties that bring
About unending joy, resulting in
Delightful daily calls, "Do it again!"
I glory in that notion, but I often
Doubt if, with all my faults, I could ever
Bring out that same enthusiasm, and
Instead exasperatingly inspire,
"Oh, not again. . ."
                      My child, I don't grow faint.
Just as my angels don't grow weary dancing
When one repents, so I will never cease
To run to you when you turn back to me.

A SON AMONG THE STARS

Then Jesus said to him, "Today salvation has come to this house, because he too is a son of Abraham." (Luke 19:9)

The stars that hung in heaven's heights released
Their light at God's command to Abraham
As sign and symbol for his family.
Their number, brightness both conveyed how God
Would give his blessing. Centuries would pass
With many Israelites forsaking their
High calling. Small Zacchaeus stood as one
Whose light had dimmed and failed to shine God's glory.
Our Lord, we're told, looked up to see the one
Who climbed above the fray that he might glimpse
The life and light who walked through Jericho.
The fallen son came near creation's source,
Caught flame again, and beamed in radiance,
And there reclaimed his place among the stars.

THE SHEPHERD

"Very truly, I tell you, anyone who does not enter the sheepfold by the gate but climbs in by another way is a thief and a bandit. The one who enters by the gate is the shepherd of the sheep." (John 10:1-2)

Those other shepherds never cared to feed
The flock, but only cared that they themselves
Were fed. They drank from waters clear as crystal,
But, unconcerned for thirsty sheep, they stepped
when leaving in the pools and muddied them.
They stood on the periphery and watched
Sheep scatter as wild animals pursued.
They never tended maimed or injured lambs.

But I will search the valleys and the hills.
I'll call my sheep, and all who hear my voice
I'll lead to vibrant streams. And for the lame
And wounded lambs, I'll bend and scoop
Them in my arms and whisper in their ears,
Come, Weary One, and I will give you rest.

DO NOT BE TERRIFIED

"When you hear of wars and insurrections, do not be terrified; for these things must take place first, but the end will not follow immediately."
(Luke 21:9)

Since their entire lives revolved around
The temple, shock most likely covered all
Their faces as their quivering voices asked
The Lord precisely when these things would be.
If nightmares are to come, a warning sign
Might help alleviate the strain they bring.
If storms are sure to knock the power out,
It would be wise to have the candles ready.

But Jesus doesn't give them what they want:
Clear signs which light the way. He simply says,
"Do not be terrified," as if to say,
The dark must come; don't let it rule your day.
Your life is not in rocks and stones but it is
In me, the light which can't be overcome.

BEING READY

"Keep awake, therefore, for you know neither the day nor the hour."
(Matthew 25:13)

I scratched out
a lot of unusable lines this week.
I'm not really sure
what the problem was.

What I do know
is that tomorrow I will return
to my favorite chair, open up
my Moleskine, and listen again.

I might even buy an oil lamp before I do.

RESEMBLING THE KING

"And the king will answer them, 'Truly I tell you, just as you did it to one of the least of these who are members of my family, you did it to me.'" (Matthew 25:40)

I found myself approaching angels standing
Around a throne; and, on its seat sat one
Whose features—all depending on the light—
Suggested something like a Lion, then
A Lamb, then, something like the Ideal Man.
His gaze was fierce, but not without compassion.
The King's arm, hand palm up, moved to his right.
He asked, "Are you, my child, to walk this way?"
I looked up sheepishly, and then away,
And shyly shrugged a mute response. The King
Declared, "My son, my heart goes out to hearts
Who yearned for me and who have clothed themselves
In robes wool-white and deeds pure gold. So come.
This way's for all whose lives resembled mine."

THE TRUE WAY INTO LIFE

Jesus said to him, "I am the way, and the truth, and the life."
(John 14:6)

I'll lead the way into my Father's house,
Retracing Adam's steps (but in reverse);
And, I assure you, friends, this road is straight
And true. You'll not find any twists or turns,
But just a well-worn path that takes you to
My Father's home, which rests on mountain heights.
And if you feel the urge to go astray,
Just step into the prints my feet have etched.

The way will bring you to a Garden's edge,
Where cherubim will sheathe their flaming sword
Permitting you to walk into its middle.
When you arrive, I'll stretch my arms out wide,
Like horizontal beams, to welcome you
And bid you eat the fruit that gives you life.

AN EASTER LAMENT

"But go, tell his disciples and Peter that he is going ahead of you to Galilee; there you will see him, just as he told you." So they went out and fled from the tomb, for terror and amazement had seized them; and they said nothing to anyone, for they were afraid. (Mark 16:7-8)

And would we ever think a day like this
Was marked with trepidation and alarm?
Where is the joy, exuberance, and bliss?
Where is the Lord who welcomes with his arms
Outstretched? But as it is, he's absent from
This telling. All we see are women, trembling,
But tasked to tell their friends that when they come
To Galilee, he'll be there for them, waiting.

The calendar says I should celebrate:
The day of resurrection has arrived.
But angst now permeates my present state,
And all attempts at joy seem so contrived.
But like the women, I am going where
You ask, and trusting you will meet me there.

A FRIEND LIKE THOMAS

Jesus said to him, "Have you believed because you have seen me? Blessed are those who have not seen and yet have come to believe." (John 20:29)

I'm prone, like Thomas, to stand fast in my
Perceived inequity, to state bluntly
My obstinate refusal: *If my eye
Doesn't see, hands don't touch, I won't comply
With your belief.* Why are there some who see
A miracle, while I go blindly praying
In faith that you will show yourself to me?
Instead, I'm walking in the darkness, groping
Along the wall. And yet, you say I'm blessed
For still believing though I haven't seen,
For trusting your divine breath has here breached
My walled-up heart, with no space in between
Us, and assuring me your love extends
Far past what eye can see to all your friends.

SEEING JESUS

When he was at the table with them, he took bread, blessed and broke it, and gave it to them. Then their eyes were opened, and they recognized him; and he vanished from their sight. (Luke 24:30-31)

I'd like to think the sun was at its peak
When they began their travels to Emmaus,
Highlighting, even in that noontime brightness,
They walked with clouded vision: eyes too weak
To see beyond their limited perceptions,
And minds too slow of heart to comprehend
How Jesus said this very tale would end,
And how he'd shatter all their expectations.

So when, at dusk, he sat with his companions,
With candles faintly shining on their meal,
Our Lord performed familiar actions
And granted them a dawning that revealed
His broken body risen from the dead,
The light for all the world, its living bread.

SITTING

"All [the disciples] were constantly devoting themselves to prayer."
(Acts 1:14)

They watched in wordless wonder as their Lord
Ascended into heaven. And who knows
How long they would have gazed agape at clouds
If angels hadn't called them back to earth.
When walking to Jerusalem, I'm sure
Silence continued as those witnesses
Discerned what life without their Lord would mean.
And here, two scenes combine: The faithful meet
Inside the upper room and share blank glances—
Suggesting answers have eluded them—
While Jesus regally approaches his
Divine throne. As disciples sit for prayer,
So Jesus sits, installed as cosmic king,
And sees, first thing, his brothers seeking him.

II. Epistles

HALF-LIFE

So you also must consider yourselves dead to sin and alive to God in Christ Jesus. (Romans 6:11)

A ghost, my soul;
a half-life straddling
the worlds of earth and heaven, called
to higher heights but settling
for muck and mire to lurch
through lesser life.

Though every taste
has soured, still I'm loathe
to let this life go, taking ease
in what is known instead of what
might be, and haunted by
that brutal act.

But, oh, that I may fully die.

THE EIGHTH DAY

So if anyone is in Christ, there is a new creation: everything old has passed away; see, everything has become new! (2 Corinthians 5:17)

And God said, "Let my Son arise!
Though we made every human holy,
they turned away; yet, we pursued them,
even unto death.
Now we will breathe new life
into their dust, in male and female—
we will re-create them all."

God blessed his Son and said,
"Tell them, 'Be fruitful and multiply.
Go to the earth's far ends in my good name.'
Behold, I've given every gift they need
so that my life and love will heal them all."
And it was so.

God looked and saw his own
belovèd Son—risen, remade—and he
was very good. So God shall likewise bless
all those remade in him:

the eighth day.

GALATIANS

So some have come and planted wicked thoughts
Suggesting you all lack what God would need
To fully bring you in his family—
They say, "The cross must bow to law and deed."
Well, I can show you this is not the way
Our Father spoke to Abraham, who said
Our faith unlocks the door to covenant.
You are the promise prophets gave: *I am,*
In days to come, renewing heart and mind,
Pouring my Spirit on all flesh to soften
Your hearts and hardened wills. You are a land
Of new creation, fruitful as a garden.
I'll tell you then the words that God would tell:
You are my children, heirs, my Israel.

STILLING THE STORM

But even if you do suffer for doing what is right, you are blessed. Do not fear what they fear, and do not be intimidated. (1 Peter 3:14)

I know it seems as if you're sailing on
A troubled sea, and riding waves of taunts
And threats beating incessantly against
Your boat, with winds suggesting storms are far
From over. Yet, recall you've passed through waters
More powerful than these, through tides God's hands
Poured over you, which seemed like death but that
Immersed you in Christ's resurrection life.
No drenching now can harm you. Do not fear
And do not give into intimidation.
If any try to plunge you in the deep,
Know Jesus' arms will surely draw you out.
And as he spoke to those rebellious spirits,
He'll call within your storm and say, "Be still."

III. Apocalypse

READING REVELATION

Blessed is the one who reads the words of the prophecy...
(Revelation 1:3)

For some, the words have been an obstacle,
Like road signs written in a foreign language.
And once distressed by John's strange spectacle
All future readings carry that past baggage.
For others, Revelation's filled with terrors—
Dire images predicting our destruction.
And some will say the world described there mirrors
Events right now, augmenting apprehension.
But what if we first read it as a story,
And set aside concern for finding meaning,
And jettison our favored scheme or theory
To step inside the tale John is presenting?
We may find more than words stamped on a page;
New meaning may appear while we're on stage.

ON WORDS

... and blessed are those who hear and who keep what is written in it; for the time is near. (Revelation 1:3)

We must test words for weight, for some are light
And airy, lacking strength to give a place
Or build a habitation for what's named.
A breeze will carry these away and we,
With watchful care, would benefit to let
Those words wisp on and dissipate like smoke,
Then search for something solid, something more
Like mountain ranges winds could never sway.

Yes, we must test each word for weight, for we
Are told that glory has a heaviness which can
Impress its mold on us if we allow
Its gravity, engrafted in the Word
Which heaven speaks, to soon inspirit us
And fill us up, that we remain unmoved.

HEAVEN: SOURCE AND CENTER

After this I looked, and there in heaven a door stood open! And the first voice, which I had heard speaking to me like a trumpet, said, "Come up here, and I will show you what must take place after this."
(Revelation 4:1)

John, come up here. Like Moses come and see
My heavenly abode and enter in
This paradox. This realm, which is the beating
Heart pulsing life across the cosmos and
The mountain from whose heights all living waters
Begin and flow. This is the world I wished
To give and share with my first "Let there be,"
Though my belovèd imagers refused.
But soon the arteries will be unclogged;
The dams which were constructed broken down.
And once released, my living waters will
Both purify and mend the world I made.
Then heaven will descend and earth be raised
To meet and be, at last, my tent of praise.

www.ingramcontent.com/pod-product-compliance
Lightning Source LLC
Chambersburg PA
CBHW060359050426
42449CB00009B/1820